John Tavener
Choral Collection

Chester Music
(A division of Music Sales Limited)
14-15 Berners Street, London W1T 3LJ, UK

CHESTER MUSIC

COMPOSER'S NOTES

Introduction

I have long regarded the writing of short choral works as an essential part of the composer's craft. In the Orthodox church, ikons provide a focus for prayer and contemplation, and in my pieces I have tried to produce ikons in sound, instead of with wood and paint. I hope that most of the present collection will be within easy reach of amateur choirs.

Many of these pieces were written in memory of people who have died, and I see them as gifts from parting souls. Thus, *Hymn to the Mother of God* was inspired by the passing of my mother, *Eonia* by the death of the visionary artist Cecil Collins, and *Song for Athene* by a tragic bicycle accident which killed a young Greek girl. This was later sung at the funeral of Diana, Princess of Wales, as her coffin was borne from Westminster Abbey. *I will lift up mine eyes unto the hills* was written in memory of the sister of my publisher, James Rushton, *Prayer to the Holy Trinity* remembers my distant ancestor, the sixteenth century composer John Taverner, and *Funeral Canticle* is to the eternal memory of my father.

1. Hymn to the Mother of God

First performance on 14th December 1985 by the Choir of Winchester Cathedral conducted by Martin Neary.

Text from the Liturgy of St Basil.

This is the first of *Two Hymns to the Mother of God* which were written in memory of my mother. It is for double choir, and it speaks of the almost cosmic power attributed to the Mother of God by the Orthodox Church.

2. Come and do Your will in me

Commissioned by The Friends of Chester Cathedral to celebrate their Diamond Jubilee. First performance on 20th June 1998, by Chester Cathedral Choir conducted by David Poulter.

Words from the *Hymn of Entry* by Archimandrite Vasileios, and from the Orthodox Liturgy.

"I do not wish, I do not desire to live long. I wish to live with You. It is You, who are long life, vital, and without end... with him in sleep, and in waking, filling his life with sweetness... not to check our plans, and hopes, and our life, but to confirm, strengthen, and bless them."

from the *Hymn of Entry*
by Archimandrite Vasileios

The music must be sung with enormous intensity and sonority, casting all into the fire of God.

3. Love Bade Me Welcome

Written for the Choir of Winchester Cathedral. Commissioned by the Dean and Chapter of Winchester Cathedral for the enthronement as Bishop of Winchester of the Right Reverend Colin James on 28th June 1985.

Words by George Herbert.

4. Annunciation

Commissioned in the name of Sir Thomas Armstrong by the Musicians Benevolent Fund, for performance at the St Cecilia's Day Service in Westminster Abbey on 25th November 1992.

Text from St Luke's Gospel.

The text of this work comes from the part of St Luke's Gospel where the Archangel Gabriel tells Mary that she is to bear the Son of God. His words are sung by the main choir, and should build up to a thunderous, awesome theophany. The response of the Mother of God 'How shall this be...' comes from a quartet of solo voices set apart, preferably raised in a gallery. By this I have tried to portray her humility, terror and total acceptance, without which the Incarnation could never have taken place.

5. Song for Athene

Commissioned by the BBC. First performance on 22nd January 1994 at St Giles in the Barbican, London, by the BBC Singers conducted by Simon Joly.

Words from Shakespeare's *Hamlet* and the Orthodox Funeral Service.

This work was written in memory of Athene Hariades, who died tragically in March 1993. Her inner and outer beauty was reflected in her love of acting, poetry, music and of the Orthodox Church. If the work is to performed at the funeral of a man, the word 'servant' may be substituted for 'hand-maid' on page 31.

6. Eonia

Commissioned for the 27th Seminar on Contemporary Choral Music, University College, Cork, Ireland, May 1990. The Seminar on Contemporary Choral Music is organised by the Abbey Life Cork International Festival, grant-aided by the Arts Council (An Chomhiarle Ealaion) in conjunction with the Music Department, University College, Cork.

Words by Seferis, and from the Gospels.

Εἴτε βραδιάζει	Whether it's dusk
εἴτε φέγγει	or dawn's first light
μένει λευκὸ	the jasmin stays
τὸ γιασεμί.	always white.

He asked for bread and we gave Him a stone...
Do whatsoever He bids you.

Господи помилуй.	Lord, have mercy

Remember me, the thief exclaimed...
The house where I was born...
This night in Paradise.

Εἴτε βραδιάζει	Whether it's dusk
εἴτε φέγγει	or dawn's first light
μένει λευκὸ	the jasmin stays
τὸ γιασεμί.	always white.

My work Αἰωνία (Eonia) is a Haiku or 'fragrance'. I opened the Collected Poems of Seferis and found Tὸ Γιασεμί – *The Jasmin*. At the same time I was talking on the telephone to Mother Thekla; I read her Tὸ Γιασεμί and she continued in English, then Slavonic and then English. It was almost like dictated writing.

I was mourning my dear friend Cecil, and Αἰωνία is a fragile tribute, to the man I loved, and to his fragile, beautiful and iconographical art.

The Greek word Αἰωνία is pronounced with the 'e' as in the 'a' of bake, and 'i' as in the 'ee' of thee.

7. Ikon of St Cuthbert of Lindisfarne

Commissioned by James Lancelot and the Choir of Durham Cathedral with funds provided by Northern Arts and the Dean and Chapter of Durham. First performance on the 1300th anniversary of the death of St Cuthbert – 20th March 1987 – by the Choir of Durham Cathedral conducted by James Lancelot.

Words by Mother Thekla.

The *Ikon of St Cuthbert of Lindisfarne* is constructed in the form of a Byzantine Canon, though it must be emphasised that it is not a true canon, but a framework for the musical structure.

IRMOS: introductory verse to put St Cuthbert into perspective in the history of salvation.

TROPARIAON 1: the name Cuthbert is derived from *Guthhertos* –worthy of God– his childhood and youth as his father's shepherd in Scotland.

TROPARION 2: the monastic call (Litany–Kyrie Eleison).

KATHISMA: the call to solitude.

TROPARION 3: tranquil and gentle, a balm on bruised hearts.

TROPARION 4: his retreat from human adulation.

TROPARION 5: hope for the world–the first hint of The Mother of God, always associated with wells.

KYRIE ELEISON/KONTAKION: stylised eulogy.

TROPARION 6: echo of the three children in the furnace overcoming all by prayer.

TROPARION 7: the meeting point of the rejoicing communion of Saints in heaven and earth.

TROPARION 8: Durham. *Dunelm* is derived from the saxon *dun*, a hill, and *holme*, a place in or surrounded by water.

Hagiography presents the life of St Cuthbert in stylised form, but his radiance shines through in its own reality. In like manner, this *Ikon of St Cuthbert*, an ikon of music and words in the place of wood and paint, seeks to recall, in its stylised form, the personal aura of Cuthbert, Saint of Lindisfarne.

8. Prayer to the Holy Trinity

Commissioned by the Cambridge Taverner Choir. First performance on 21st April 1996, at Jesus College Chapel, Cambridge, by the Cambridge Taverner Choir conducted by Owen Rees.

Text: Orthodox Prayer.

This prayer is the foundation of Orthodox faith in the Holy Trinity. In setting it to music, I have tried to capture something of the deep compunction and repentance which lie at the heart of Orthodoxy. Each person of the Trinity is represented by a different tone in the Byzantine "ochtoechos". The semichorus should be placed at a considerable distance from the main choir. It is like the "heatbeat" of repentance.

In the Roman Catholic Church, the Holy Spirit is deemed to come from both the Father and the Son, but this is regarded as a heresy by the Orthodox: we believe that the spirit proceeds only from the Father. For this reason counterpoint is forbidden in Orthodox church music, as it is considered a symbol of dualism, and I have reflected this in my setting. The Roman Catholic John Taverner (c.1495–1545) was imprisoned for heresy, but was later reprieved for "being but a musitian".

9. I will lift up mine eyes unto the hills

Commissioned for the opening of the 1990 City of London Festival. First performance on 8th July 1990 by the Choir of St Paul's Cathedral conducted by John Scott.

Text: Psalm 121.

10. Funeral Canticle

Text from the Orthodox Funeral Service, and by Mother Thekla.

Funeral Canticle was written in loving memory of my father. Such was his love of life and people that he constantly surprised us by rallying round when he was thought to be at the point of death. So I wrote this work during the last year of my father's life, in preparation for the interdenominational funeral service which was his wish.

My father's funeral was celebrated by Archbishop Gregorios of Thayateira and Great Britain, Archimandrite Father Ephrem and Arch-priest Father Michael Fortunatto, as well as three Pastors from the United Reformed Church, which was the Church of my father's baptism. It was a moving ceremony, with ikons, and candles lighting up the church, and I believe it would have delighted the man who lay in the open coffin. Eternal memory — Kenneth.

Performance Notes

Αἰωνία ἡ μνήμη etc. should be sung in Byzantine manner, and the soloist must familiarise himself with this style of singing. If wished, the *Kliros* section may be doubled by a string quartet or small group of strings. Parts are available on hire from the publisher.

Αἰωνία ἡ μνήμη. *(Eternal memory.)*

We are born as naked infants,
Then baptised into Christ our God,
Rocks and shoals of life beset us,
Washed in waters of our Lord. *Alleluia.*

We must run the course that tempts us,
With the idols of the world,
Yet we have our Lord and master,
And His mother for our shield. *Alleluia.*

Grant, O Lord in love unceasing,
Rest to him* now lying here,
Grant him* rest among the faithful,
In the life beyond compare. *Alleluia.*

(KLIROS)

What earthly sweetness remaineth unmixed with grief?
What glory standeth immutable on earth?
All things are but shadows most feeble, but most deluding dreams:
Yet one moment only, and death shall supplant them all.
But in the light of thy countenance, O Christ, and in the sweetness of Thy beauty,
Give rest to him* whom thou hast chosen,
Because Thou lovest mankind.

Αἰωνία αὐτόυ† ἡ μνήμη. *(Eternal memory to him.)*

* him; her; them; as appropriate
† αὐτόυ (him); αὐτῆς (her); αὐτῶν (them); as appropriate

Pronunciation guide for the Greek text:

Ai	as French <u>é</u>clat	αὐ	as French <u>a</u>ffecter
ω	as French <u>o</u>ncle	τόυ	as English <u>too</u>
νί	as English <u>knee</u>	τῆς	as English <u>teas</u>
α	as French l<u>a</u>	τῶν	as French <u>ton</u>
		ἡ μνήμη	"eem nee mee"

Alleluia should be pronounced in the Greek orthodox manner:

A	as in French l<u>a</u>
lle	"lee"
lu	"loo"
i	"ee"
a	"ya" with short a, as in French l<u>a</u>

J.T.

Order No. CH 61599
This collection © Copyright 2000 Chester Music Ltd.

Cover design by Michael Bell Design
Photograph by Guy Hills
Music processing:
    Nos. 1, 3, 4, 5, 7 by Chris Hinkins
    Nos. 2 and 6 by Music Copying Services (South Wales)
    No. 8 by Musography
    Nos. 9 and 10 by New Notations London

in memory of my Mother – Eternal memory!

HYMN TO THE MOTHER OF GOD

John Tavener

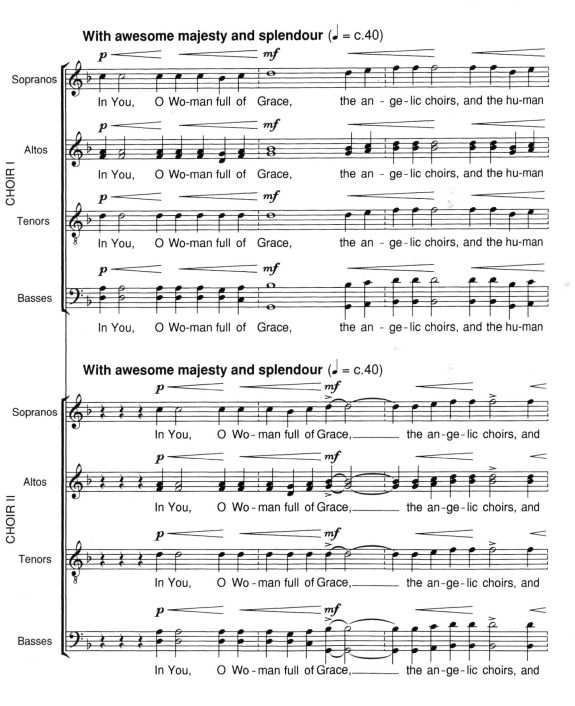

4

COME AND DO YOUR WILL IN ME

Archimandrite Vasileios

John Tavener

Serene and gentle

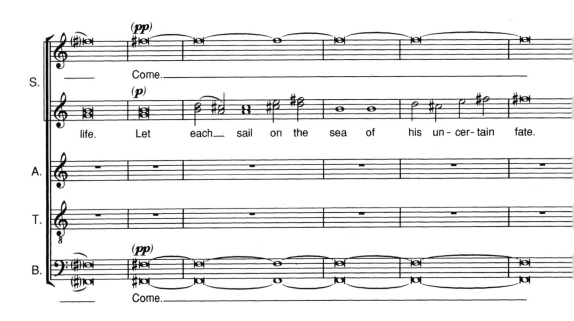

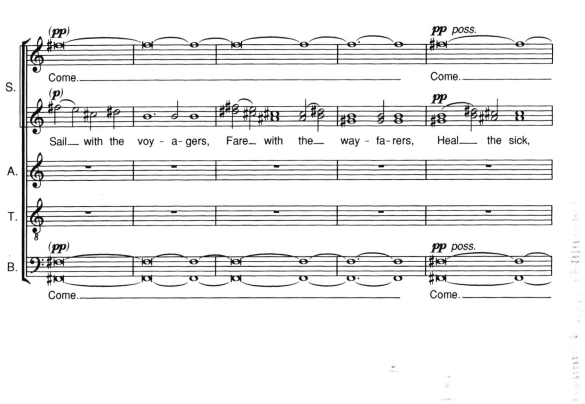

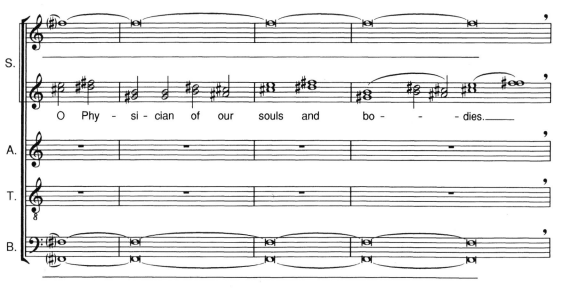

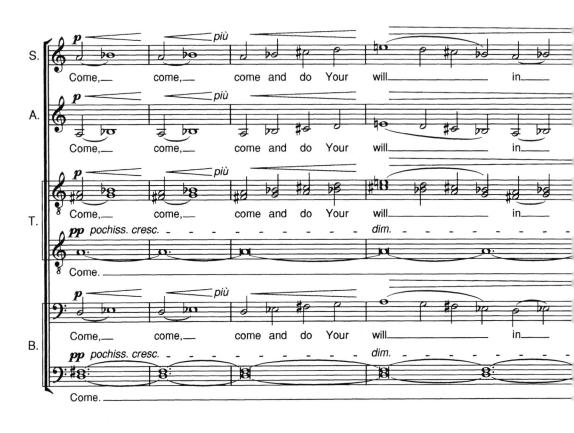

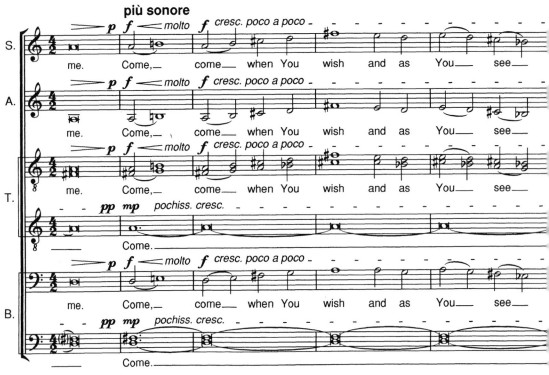

14

Pigadaki
28th October, 1997

to Robin Boyle

LOVE BADE ME WELCOME

George Herbert

John Tavener

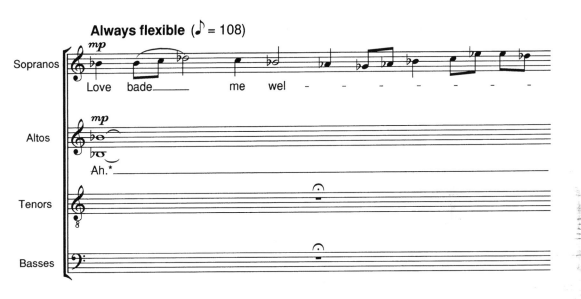

* Breathe when necessary, but not simultaneously

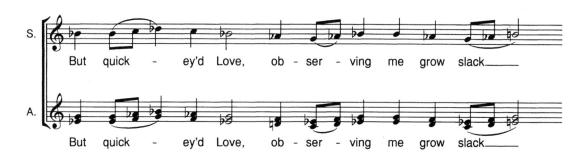

But quick - ey'd Love, ob - ser - ving me grow slack

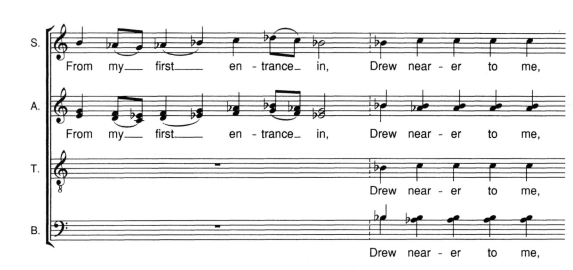

From my first en - trance in, Drew near - er to me,

poco rit. **Broadly**

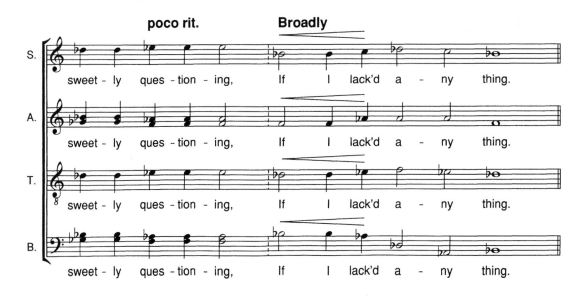

sweet - ly ques - tion - ing, If I lack'd a - ny thing.

17

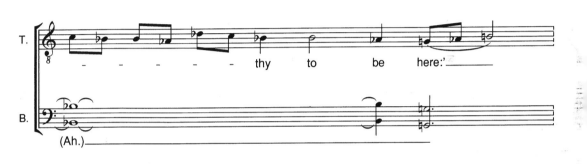

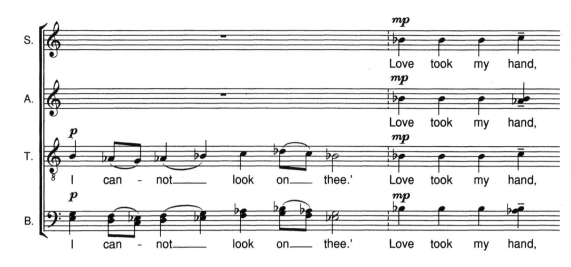

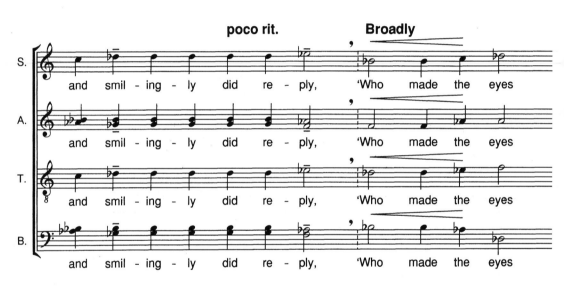

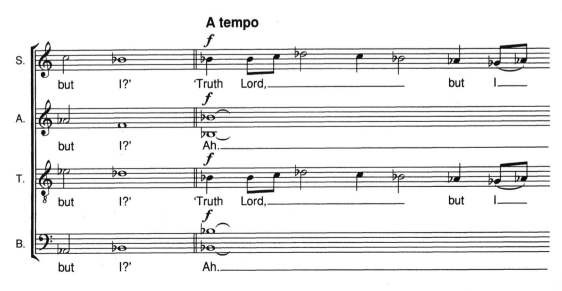

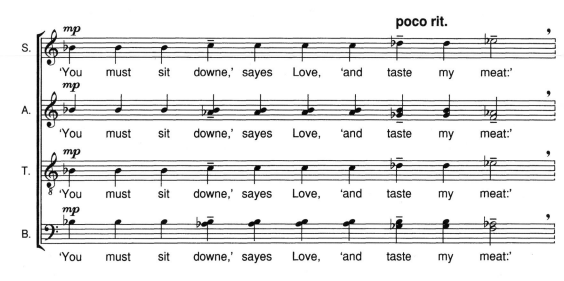

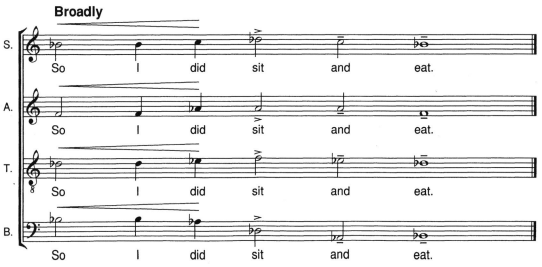

for the Musicians Benevolent Fund

ANNUNCIATION

John Tavener

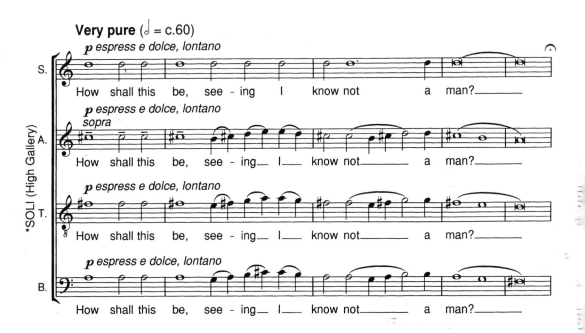

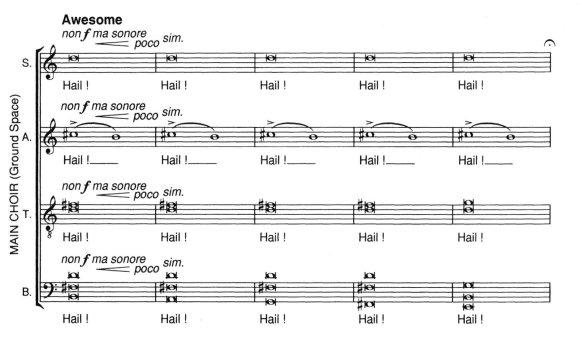

* Soloists are preferred, but a semi-chorus may be substituted if necessary.

22

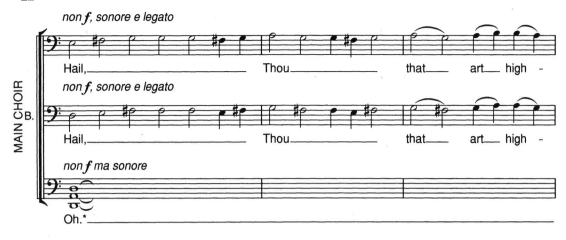

Very pure

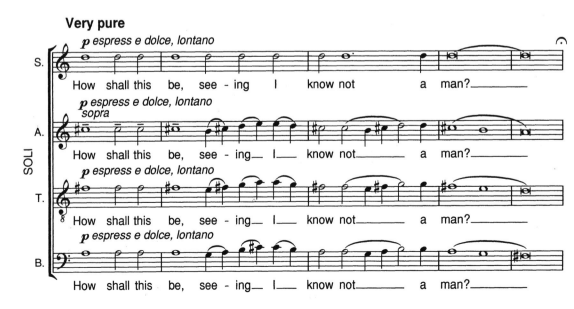

* 'Oh' as in the 'o' of 'log'. Breathe when necessary but not simultaneously.

More awesome, thunderous

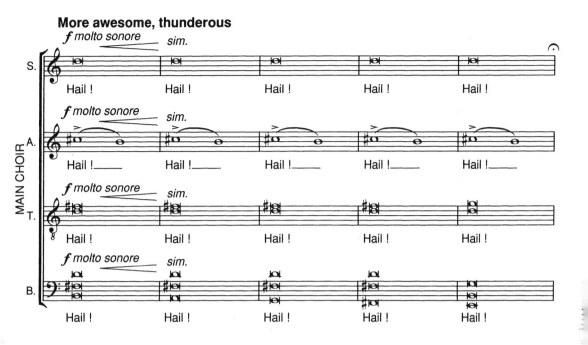

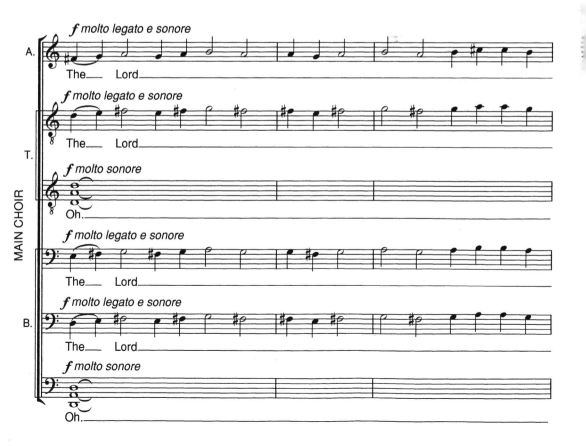

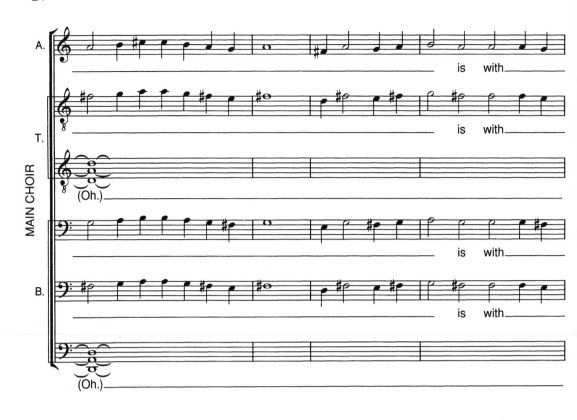

Very pure

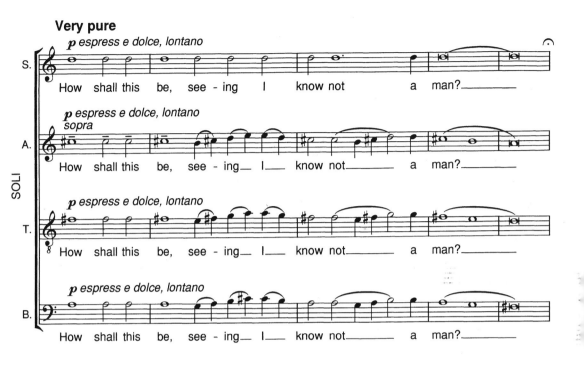

SOLI

S. How shall this be, see-ing I know not a man?

A. How shall this be, see-ing I know not a man?

T. How shall this be, see-ing I know not a man?

B. How shall this be, see-ing I know not a man?

Very awesome, thunderous

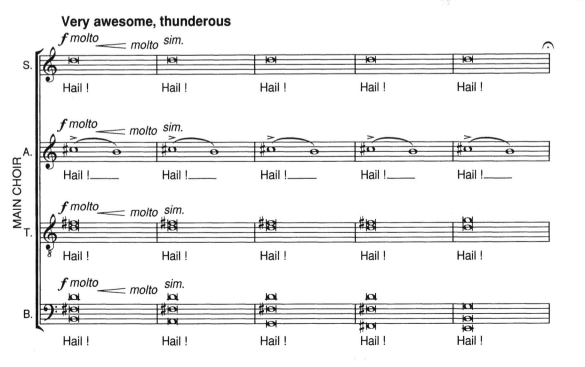

MAIN CHOIR

S. Hail! Hail! Hail! Hail! Hail!

A. Hail! Hail! Hail! Hail! Hail!

T. Hail! Hail! Hail! Hail! Hail!

B. Hail! Hail! Hail! Hail! Hail!

26

Radiant

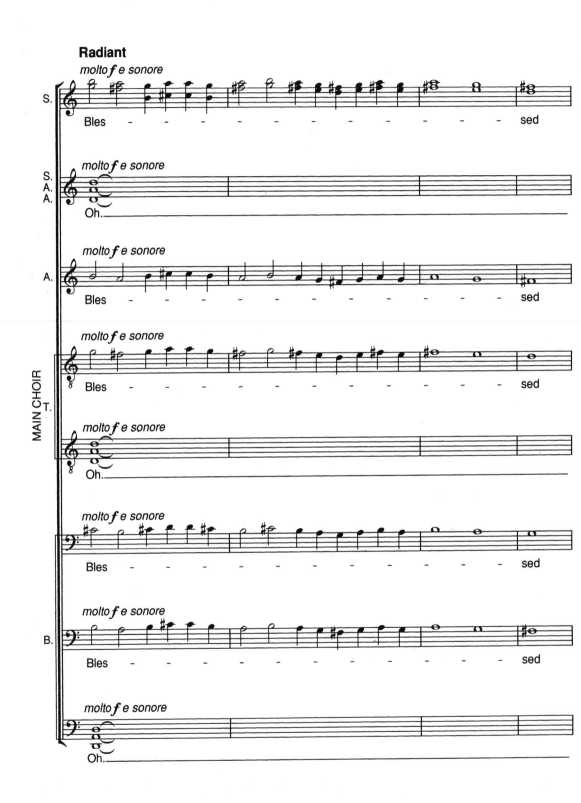

N aldretts
Sunday of the Cross
29th March 1992

eternal memory – Cecil Collins

Αἰωνία...

Eonia . . .

John Tavener

With unearthly stillness and purity, without expression

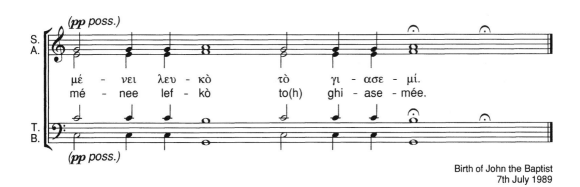

Birth of John the Baptist
7th July 1989

SONG FOR ATHENE

John Tavener

Very tender, with great inner stillness and serenity
(♩ = c. 56-60)

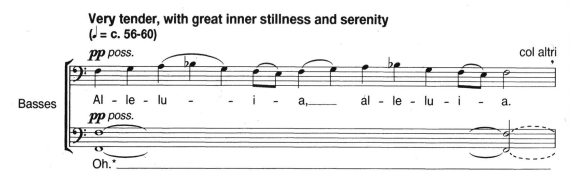

* 'Oh' as in the 'o' of 'log'. Breathe when necessary, but not simultaneously.

34

With resplendent joy in the Resurrection

Bermuda/Naldretts
11th April 1993

to Mother Thekla

IKON OF SAINT CUTHBERT
OF LINDISFARNE

John Tavener

IRMOS

Is - ra - el passed dry shod through the sea,

and your foot - steps trod the sands of Lin - dis - farne.

REFRAIN

Ho - ly Fa - ther, Cuth-bert of Lin - dis - farne, pray to God for us.

TROPARION 1

Tranquil

Wor-thy of God, you pas-tured your Fa-ther's flocks on bar-ren moun-tain rid -ges.

REFRAIN

Ho - ly Fa - ther, Cuth-bert of Lin - dis - farne, pray to God for us.

TROPARION 2

Poco più, ma sempre tranquillo

Your mas - ter called you a - way to feed

his— flocks, hun - - - gry for hea - ven - ly bread.

REFRAIN

sempre p

Ho - ly Fa - ther, Cuth-bert of Lin - dis - farne,— pray to God— for— us.

Tenor Solo

Quickly, between speech and singing,
in the manner of an Orthodox reader

sing the phrase 11 times   **A tempo**

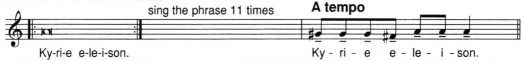

Ky-ri-e e-le-i-son.   Ky - ri - e e - le - i - son.

KATHISMA

molto f sonore

Bar - ren— is - land, de - - - so -late, slate - clothed wa - -

-ters surge— on— the rocks!

REFRAIN

sempre p

Ho - ly Fa - ther, Cuth-bert of Lin - dis - farne,— pray to God— for— us.

TROPARION 3

Liquid and tranquil

Monk and— Fa - ther of souls,— your tears— of con-tri -tion flowed in-to

wa-ters of heal - - - ing for all who sought your____ help.

REFRAIN

sempre p

Ho-ly Fa-ther, Cuth-bert of Lin-dis-farne,____ pray to God__ for__ us.

TROPARION 4

Steely

poco f

You hid the sweet__ scent of your beau - ty with-in the thorns

of so - li - tude, tire - less as - ce - tic la - bour.

REFRAIN

sempre p

Ho-ly Fa-ther, Cuth-bert of Lin-dis-farne,____ pray to God__ for__ us.

TROPARION 5

Flowing

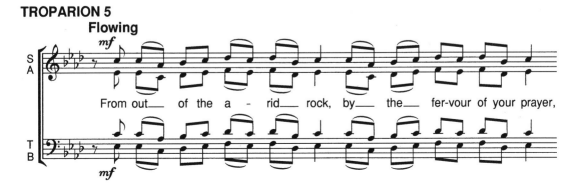

mf

From out__ of the a - rid__ rock, by__ the__ fer-vour of your prayer,

mf

38

the well - spring gushed forth of pu - rest wa - - - ter.

REFRAIN

Ho - ly Fa - ther, Cuth-bert of Lin - dis-farne, pray to God for us.

Tenor Solo

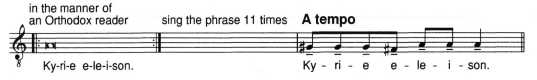

Ky - ri-e e-le-i-son.   Ky - ri - e e - le - i - son.

KONTAKION

Won - der - wor - ker of Bri - tain, you lived, a de - sert dwel - ler,

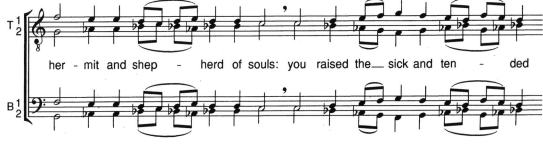

her - mit and shep - herd of souls: you raised the sick and ten - ded

the poor, and made bar-ley to spring from dry soil.

TROPARION 6

Più

As the three child-ren sang be-dewed in the fur-nace, so you, O Ho-ly one, sang prai-ses to God in the waves of the sea.

REFRAIN

sempre p

Ho-ly Fa-ther, Cuth-bert of Lin-dis-farne, pray to God for us.

TROPARION 7

With majesty

più sempre: molto f e sonore

A-pos-tles and pa-tri-archs, pro-phets and

A-pos-tles and pa-tri-archs, pro-phets and

Ah.*

* Breathe when necessary

monks, sing in praise of your life: and let us, the people, unite in song:

monks, sing in praise of your life: and let us, the people, unite in song:

(Ah.) Ah.

praise the Lord and exalt Him unto ages of ages.

praise the Lord and exalt Him unto ages of ages.

(Ah.)

REFRAIN

sempre p

Holy Father, Cuthbert of Lindisfarne, pray to God for us.

TROPARION 8

Serene and still

pp sempre

Your life was ever close to the water,

pp sempre

Your life was ever close to the water,

pp sempre

Ah.

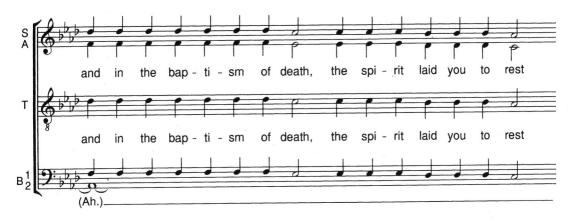

and in the bap - ti - sm of death, the spi - rit laid you to rest

and in the bap - ti - sm of death, the spi - rit laid you to rest

(Ah.)

in peace___ on the hill u - pon the wa - - ters.

in peace___ on the hill u - pon the wa - - ters.

(Ah.)

REFRAIN

sempre p

Ho - ly Fa - ther, Cuth - bert of Lin - dis - farne, ___ pray to God ___ for ___ us.

più f

Glory be to the Father, and to the Son, and to the Ho - ly Spi - - rit.

più f

eternal memory - John Taverner (c.1495 - 1545)
"being but a Musitian"

PRAYER TO THE HOLY TRINITY

John Tavener

With the deepest compunction and sobriety throughout (♩ = c.50)

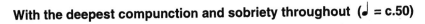

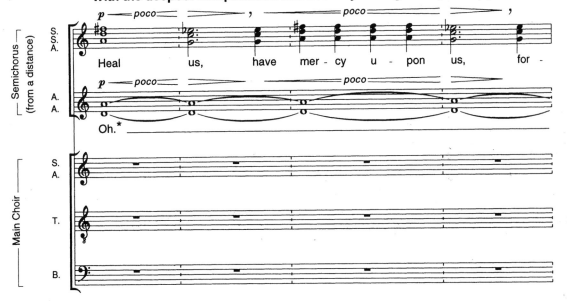

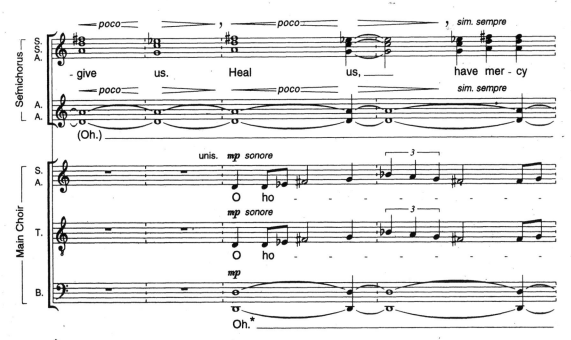

* 'Oh' as in the 'o' of 'log'. Breathe when necessary, but not simultaneously.

44

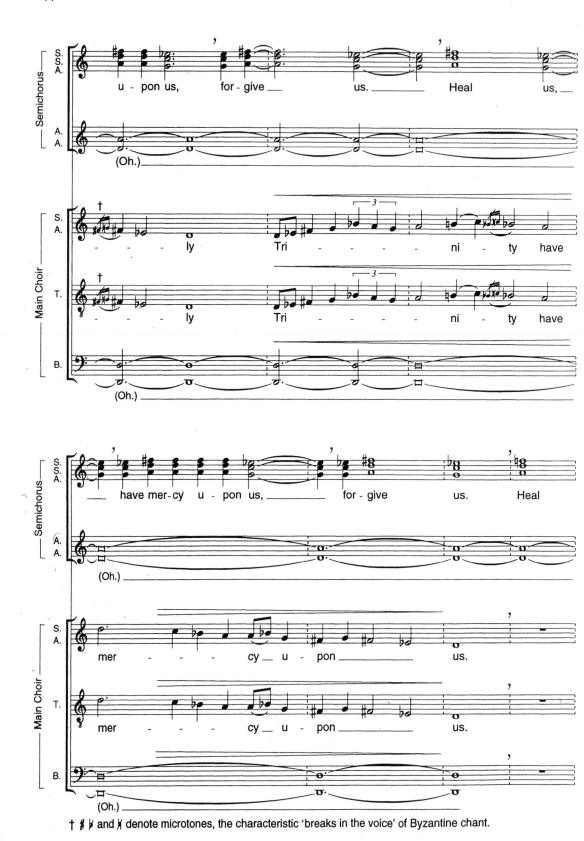

† ♯ ♭ and ✗ denote microtones, the characteristic 'breaks in the voice' of Byzantine chant.

48

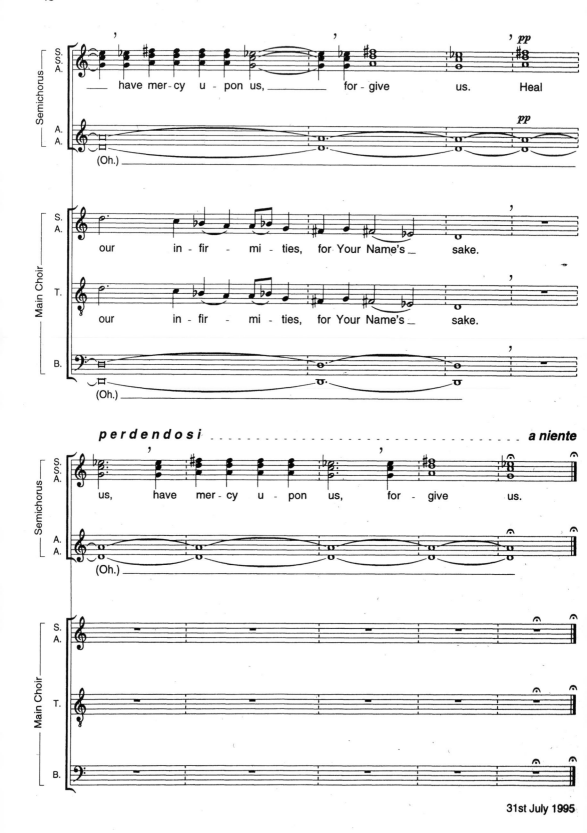

perdendosi . . . . *a niente*

31st July 1995

eternal memory - Elizabeth

I WILL LIFT UP MINE EYES
UNTO THE HILLS

John Tavener

* 'Oh' as in the 'o' of 'log'. Breathe when necessary, but not simultaneously.

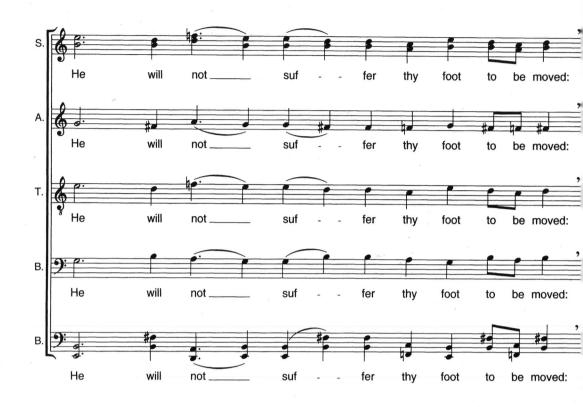

S. He will not _____ suf - - fer thy foot to be moved:

A. He will not _____ suf - - fer thy foot to be moved:

T. He will not _____ suf - - fer thy foot to be moved:

B. He will not _____ suf - - fer thy foot to be moved:

B. He will not _____ suf - - fer thy foot to be moved:

a little more gentle and tender

c.4"

S. he that kee - peth thee will not slum - ber.

A. he that kee - peth thee will not slum - ber.

T. he that kee - peth thee will not slum - ber.

B. he that kee - peth thee will not slum - ber.

B. he that kee - peth thee will not slum - ber.

eternal memory – Kenneth

FUNERAL CANTICLE

John Taven

Very slow (♩ = c.36)
Solemn, declaimed in Byzantine style

Sing 4 times altogether
con rubato

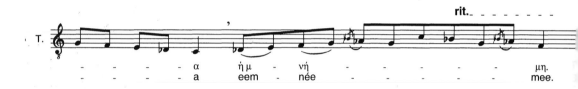

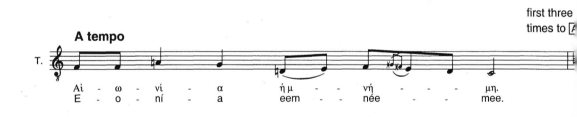

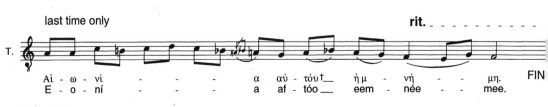

† see Preface
* Ⱦ and ⱦ denote microtones, the characteristic "breaks in the voice" of Byzantine chant.

© Copyright 1999 Chester Music Ltd.

A tempo

A **Serene and tender**

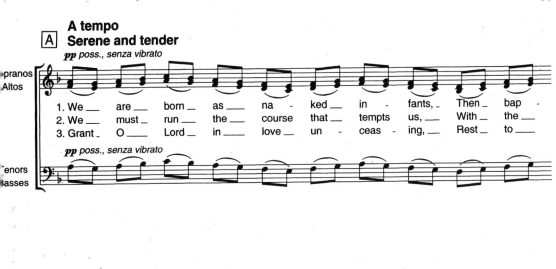

Sopranos / Altos — *pp poss., senza vibrato*

Tenors / Basses — *pp poss., senza vibrato*

1. We — are — born — as — na - ked — in - fants, — Then — bap -
2. We — must — run — the — course that — tempts us, — With — the —
3. Grant — O — Lord in — love — un - ceas - ing, — Rest — to —

- tised — in - to Christ — our — God, Rocks — and — shoals — of — life —
i - dols — of — the — world, Yet — we — have — our — Lord —
him* — now — ly - ing — here, Grant — him* — rest — a - mong —

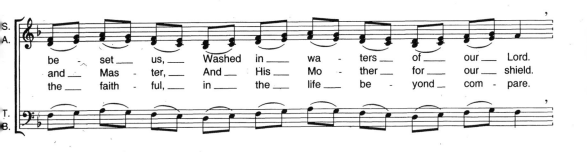

be - set — us, — Washed in — wa - ters — of — our — Lord.
and — Mas - ter, — And — His — Mo - ther — for — our — shield.
the — faith - ful, — in — the — life — be - yond — com - pare.

Al - le - lu - ia. Al - le - lu - ia. Al - le - lu - - - - i - - a.

* see Preface

B KLIROS

* see Preface

D.C.
1996